MW01487487

Just Got **Engaged!**

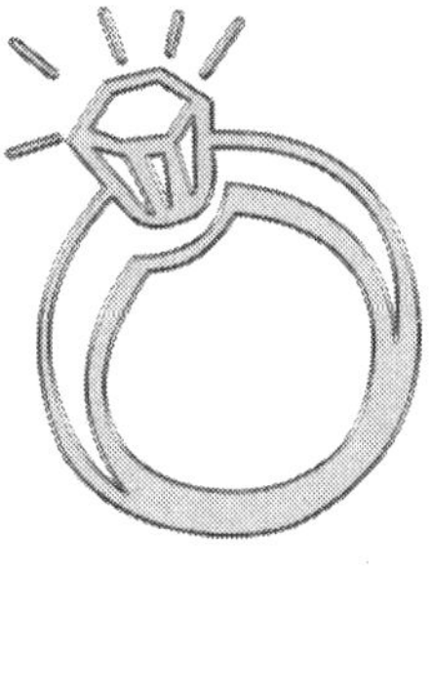

Made in the USA
Columbia, SC
10 December 2019

84645473R00074